Blanche Saunders:

DOG CARE

FOR BOYS AND GIRLS

Drawings by Haris Petie

1971—Fifth Printing

HOWELL BOOK HOUSE, 845 THIRD AVENUE
NEW YORK, N.Y. / 10022

TO BOYS AND GIRLS

If you love your dog you will want to train him and give him good care. Training has been thoroughly covered in *Dog Training for Boys and Girls*. *Dog Care for Boys and Girls* tells you how to feed, groom, and bathe your dog. There are tips on how to keep your dog healthy; what to do in an emergency; how to recognize parasites. You will learn about dog shows, obedience, and field trials. You will discover many things about dogs that you never knew before.

CONTENTS

Your Puppy's First Day 7

Rules of the Game 11

Things to Remember 15

Feeding Your Dog 19

What's for Dinner? 20

How Much? 22

Feeding Tips 23

More about Feeding 24

Grooming 26

Worms and How to Recognize Them 30

External Parasites and How to Recognize *Them* 32

Bathing Your Dog 34

Baths Made Easy 35

Keeping Your Dog Healthy 37

The Sick Dog 39

Trouble Signs 41

Rules for the Sick Room 42

How to Give Medicine 43

Accidents and the Unusual 44

More Health Tips 47

Your Dog's Medicine Chest 49

How to Muzzle Your Dog   50

How to Lift Your Dog   51

How to Tie Your Dog   52

How to Weigh Your Dog   53

Your Dog's Bed   54

Sweater? Raincoat?   55

Car Sickness   56

The Female Dog   57

Dog Shows   58

How a Dog Becomes a Breed Champion   62

How a Dog Gets into the Group   65

How a Dog Is Named Best Dog in Show   66

How a Dog Becomes an Obedience Champion   68

Dog Show Rules   71

Dog Show Ribbons   74

Sanctioned Matches   75

Junior Showmanship Classes   75

Traveling with Your Dog   76

Before You Leave on Vacation   78

Dog Tips—Dog Sense—Some Interesting Facts   80

Parts of Your Dog's Body   84

Dog Professions   85

Dog Diary—Dog Records   86

If your puppy could talk, he would probably say, "This has been an exciting day." He might even add, "I'm rather sleepy. Think I'll take a nap." When your puppy doesn't want to play, don't force him. Puppies are like babies—they sleep more than they stay awake.

If your puppy didn't eat the dinner you so carefully prepared, blame it on the toys you bought him or on his inquisitive nature. Adventure and curiosity are a part of every puppy's make-up.

[7]

You found a tooth on the floor? That could very well be!
Puppies change teeth, just like people. The baby tooth you
found made room for a permanent one.

And that wart on his face was there when you bought the
puppy. You just didn't notice it in your excitement of getting
a new playmate.

The small swelling on your puppy's tummy (if there is a swelling) is called a hernia, probably caused at birth. If it doesn't disappear, ask your veterinarian about it later.

Perhaps you are wondering where the puppy will sleep! Why not put him in the bathroom with papers on the floor. A play-pen or a wire cage would be even better. If you tie the puppy, use a leather collar, a chain leash and *don't* leave him alone.

After your puppy has been in his new home fifteen or twenty minutes, take him outside for exercise. This will teach him to stay clean in the house.

And in case he is thirsty, give him a drink of water.

Puppies puddle without warning. They cry when you leave them. They chew. They bring up their dinner from excitement. Be patient! Don't give in to the puppy and don't become annoyed, and before long you will think he has lived with you always!

Never call your dog and then spank him. When he does something wrong, go to him. Hold him by the collar; then scold or give him a shaking.

Don't *yell* at your dog. The right tone is more effective. Besides, dogs don't like to be yelled at.

COME!

Never *chase* your dog to catch him. Kneel; then coax him to come by tapping the floor or the ground.

Never *grab* for your dog. Reach for him slowly, and pick him up gently.

Avoid games where your dog nips in play. Biting can become serious.

Be consistent! If it is wrong one time, it is wrong another.

Never *pull* things from your dog. Tell him, "Out!" Pry his jaws apart, then pat him after he lets go.

Never *tease*. Play in a nice way.

And when your dog has been good, give him a reward.

THINGS TO REMEMBER

Dogs get hungry as people do. Feed your puppy at regular hours, and give him a well-balanced diet. Mother can advise you on this.

Give him fresh clean water and exercise daily. In summer, change his water *twice* a day.

In fly season, spray your dog or keep him indoors. Flies annoy dogs as well as people.

Teach your puppy while he is young to stay alone so he won't bark and chew when you leave him. A wire cage is the safest place.

Give him a bone, but only the shin or knuckle variety that won't splinter. Or you can give him a strip of rawhide which can be bought at a pet shop.

Don't leave your dog without shade in summer.

Don't make him sleep where it is cold or damp.

Roll up the car windows when you take him riding. When your dog must be left in a parked car, have the car parked in the shade and open the windows slightly so he can't jump out and so he cannot suffocate.

If you tie your dog to a stake, don't leave his leash dangling; he could choke on it.

Don't use a collar that will slip too easily over your dog's head.

Above all, *train* your dog to obey you. Other people will like him better, and it will help keep him safe.

When a puppy is small, dinnertime comes often, unless you use the self-feeding method and food is kept before the puppy all the time. Here are some general rules for feeding:

3 months or under . . . . 3 to 4 times a day
3 to 6 months . . . . 2 to 3 times a day
6 months to 1 year . . . . 1 to 2 times a day
1 year and over . . . . Once a day.

This is a good schedule for the young puppy:

8 or 9 A.M. . . . . Milk and cereal.
Noon . . . . Meat and cereal with extras.
4 to 5 P.M. . . . . Same as at 8 A.M.
7 to 8 P.M. . . . . Same as at noon.

When your puppy goes on three meals a day, feed him milk in the morning. Give a solid meal at noon and again during the early evening. When he goes on two meals a day, feed milk in the morning and the solid meal during the late afternoon.

WHAT'S FOR DINNER?

Meat	Meal	Biscuit	Milk

Eggs	Fat	Cod Liver Oil	Vitamins

Dicalcium Phosphate

Meat can be fed raw or cooked. It can be ground up or in chunks, or it can come from a can. Select the kind of meat your dog likes but don't give him pork.

Meal and biscuit can be fed dry or they can be moistened with hot water. Most dog meals are a complete dog food and all you have to do is add fat.

Milk is fed to young puppies because they need the calcium, but if your older dog likes milk, it won't hurt him.

Give one egg two or three times a week, but cook it or feed just the yolk. Raw egg white contains albumen, and this is not good for dogs.

Cod liver oil is important in winter. In summer, sunshine supplies the vitamin D that every dog must have.

Your choice of fats include lard, butter, cooking oils, bacon drippings or fatty trimmings.

Dicalcium phosphate builds strong bones and helps quiet nerves.

A one-a-day vitamin pill should fill your dog's vitamin needs.

HOW MUCH?

Is your dog:

Very small?　Small?　Medium?　Large?　Very large?
The amount of food needed will vary according to your dog's size:

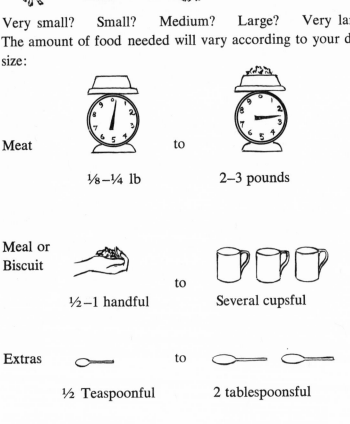

Meat   to

⅛–¼ lb   2–3 pounds

Meal or
Biscuit
                        to

½–1 handful   Several cupsful

Extras   to

½ Teaspoonful   2 tablespoonsful

Ask the person from whom you bought your dog how much food to give him, both as a puppy and as a grown dog.

As your puppy grows, so must the amount of food you give him. Feel your dog's body. Do his ribs and hip bones stick out? If so, increase his dinner! If his bones are hard to find, cut down a little. A healthy dog should be in good weight, neither too fat nor too thin.

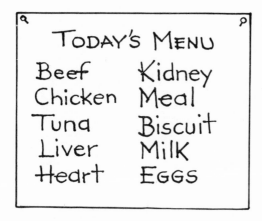

TODAY'S MENU

Dogs thrive on an unvaried diet, but if you want to give your dog a change, feed cooked oatmeal, cooked rice, cottage cheese, cooked beef hearts, liver, tripe or mutton. Feed cooked fish and chicken, but be sure there are no bones.

A dog should clean his plate within a few minutes. If your dog leaves some of his dinner, try feeding him two meals a day of smaller amounts. Perhaps he will like it better.

MORE ABOUT FEEDING

Canned dog food comes in the form of pure meat or in the form of a "ration." The meat should be mixed with meal or biscuit or some other cereal, such as cooked oatmeal or shredded wheat. The ration is a complete dog food by itself.

If milk gives your dog diarrhea, substitute chicken or beef broth.

You may not like fat but your dog will, and he should have fat.

One "fast" day a week (like going without candy) will help your dog have a good appetite. This means going without food entirely, *including tid-bits.*

When a dog eats such things as sticks, stones, dirt or animal droppings, something may be lacking in his diet, or it can be a more serious trouble sign. If your dog craves the unusual, consult your veterinarian because the dog may have something wrong organically.

Feed your puppy at regular hours. Feed your older dog at the family's convenience, but not from the table.

Water? Keep it available at all times, unless your dog is sick or you are having house-breaking problems and water is being limited.

Ice water in hot weather, is something your dog will appreciate anywhere at any time. Carry a thermos with you in the car during the summer.

As a final reminder, don't forget your dog's cracker or biscuit at bedtime. Dogs like to eat before going to sleep too.

Keep the water dish from being tipped over.

Keep the water pan cool and free of dust and insects.

GROOMING YOUR DOG

So, your dog has short hair! Groom him twice a week anyway. Use a damp sponge and wipe the dust from his coat. Brush him with a stiff brush or use a grooming mitt that slips over your hand. A hack-saw blade will help to remove dead hair.

For long-haired breeds, you need a brush, a long-toothed comb and a carder. Break the mats apart with your fingers, then comb to the skin. Cutting the mats leaves the coat uneven.

You may need help, but when you groom your dog, take care of other important things. Otherwise, it is like washing your face and leaving a dirty neck.

Clean his eyes with a piece of cotton dipped in warm water.
Caked eyelids cause sores.

Pull out what hair you can from his ears, using your thumb and
first finger. If the ears are dirty, clean them by wrapping a piece
of cotton around your finger then dipping it in alcohol. B.F.I.
powder (you can get this at the drugstore) is a good antiseptic.
Use it to prevent ear trouble.

Snip off the pointed ends of the toenails with a nail cutter. Use
a file to shorten them even more. Be careful not to make the
nails bleed.

Tartar, the dark brown substance on the teeth, can be taken off with a scaler, the kind your dentist uses. To keep your dog's teeth clean and his gums healthy, rub them once or twice a week with tooth paste or cotton dipped in Milk of Magnesia.

Does your dog have a bad breath? Wash his teeth and gums with ALKALOL (not alcohol). He will smell much sweeter.

Shorten the hair under the tail of your long-haired breed so he won't have trouble going to the bathroom. Otherwise he might get sick or have painful sores.

Cut away wads of matted hair or chewing gum from between the dog's paws. Remember what it felt like when you had to walk on stubble or had a stone in your shoe?

Grooming your dog is not only fun; it is a privilege. Start by using the right tools. Someone who specializes in your breed can tell you what brushes and combs to buy.

Have a regular place to do the grooming. Your dog will then know what to expect.

Stand your dog (unless he is a very large dog) on a steady work-bench or table. Help him feel secure.

Make him behave. If he struggles, hold him firmly until he stops struggling, then brush and comb him again.

During the grooming, check for skin trouble. Skin trouble is caused by an allergic reaction to insect bites, food, faulty diets, external irritants, fungus and bacterial infections, and many other causes. When you notice the least bit of skin irritation, take your dog to the veterinarian immediately. If you don't, the dog might be in for real trouble.

If your dog scratches, look for fleas, lice or ticks. If he is free from parasites, look for something the dog might be allergic to—his food, shampoo, or whatever you use to clean his sleeping quarters.

WORMS AND
HOW TO RECOGNIZE THEM

Not every dog has worms but *can* get them. Here are the most common:

Roundworms: You can recognize roundworms immediately. They are from two to five inches long, and they have a firm, round body, almost white in color.

Tapeworms: You won't see the whole tapeworm unless your dog was wormed for tapeworm and he passed one. Watch for segments. You will find these in the stool or on the hair under his tail. One-eighth to one-fourth inch long, pinkish-white when passed, they turn to a light brown when exposed to air. Tapeworm segments when dry remind one of little grains of rice.

It takes an expert to recognize *hookworms* and *whipworms*. They are no larger than a hair. For positive identification, your dog's stool must be examined under a microscope. Your veterinarian can do this.

Heartworms are not as common as the four we have mentioned, but they can be serious. The blood, instead of the stool, is tested. A dog with heartworm may have trouble breathing and he is usually very thin. Where the other worms live in the intestines, heartworms live in the heart, as the name implies.

Here are some things you can do to help keep your dog free of worms:

Have the dog's stool checked at regular intervals and worm him when necessary.

Disinfect and keep the dog's living quarters clean.

Use a spray to repel flies and mosquitoes. Dogs get worms from insects and animal droppings.

Get rid of fleas. This means a bath for your dog and a change of bedding.

If your dog is confined to a small outdoor run, pick up the stools daily. A toy rake and shovel will do the job just fine.

EXTERNAL PARASITES
AND HOW TO RECOGNIZE THEM

Fleas are brown and they move very fast. Look for them on your dog's head and stomach.

Lice are small, gray in color and difficult to see. They are usually found on the dog's ears and the sides of his face. Don't worry about dog lice getting on people. If they do, they never stay.

Ticks have four legs on each side of their body. Male ticks are brown and rather small. Female ticks are grayish tan, and when they are ready to lay eggs they are sometimes as big as a grape.

Use Pearson's Creolin in the bath water to rid your dog of fleas and lice. Don't make the solution too strong, and be careful of the eyes.

For a tick remedy, ask your veterinarian or local pet shop owner to recommend some product. An ordinary bath won't kill ticks.

In tick season, feel through your dog's coat every day. When you find a tick, hold it close to the head with a pair of tweezers and *shake* it loose. Destroy it; don't throw it away!

BATHING YOUR DOG

Every dog should have a bath when he gets dirty or if he has parasites. Take these precautions:

If your dog has long hair, comb him first. A matted coat never looks clean because you can't get the soap out.

Put cotton in his ears and a drop of castor oil or some vaseline in his eyes to protect them.

Have the water warm and no higher than the dog's elbows.

Use a rubber mat so he won't slip.

Use a mild shampoo so as not to irritate the skin or hurt the eyes. Nothing is better than pure castile soap. If your dog has fleas, add Pearson's Creolin to the bath water and wash around his neck first so the fleas can't run to his head. Be extra careful to protect the eyes.

Rinse the coat thoroughly to remove all soap.

After the bath, take the cotton from your dog's ears, dry him with a hair dryer or rub him briskly with towels in the hot sun.

Keep him warm for at least two hours, especially in winter.

A flat, wiping sponge, like the one mother uses to wash the dishes, is just right for washing your dog's face. Buy one for your dog, and put his name on it. Use the sponge also to cover his eyes to protect them from soap.

Use a thick sponge to remove water from his coat before you towel him. Your dog will dry quicker and you won't need so many towels.

If your dog has long hair and you want him to shake, blow in his ear and duck. Otherwise you will get a showery bath.

Skunk? Pour a can of tomato juice over your dog after you bathe him, let it dry, and rinse the coat thoroughly. Tomato juice will take skunk odor off the dog but not off his leather collar.

To keep your dog healthy, have him examined by a veterinarian at regular intervals. Ask about distemper, hepatitis, leptospirosis and rabies shots. And don't forget the booster shot that every dog should have once a year.

Don't let your dog sniff strange dogs or where dogs have been.

Disinfect your dog's feeding dish and his water pan. Wash them in very hot water to which a detergent has been added.

If you have been near a sick dog, wash your hands and change your clothes before you go near your dog. Germs are easily carried from one place to another.

THE SICK DOG

This is how you will know if your dog is sick:

He will be more quiet than usual.

He will act droopy.

He may refuse to eat or will eat very little.

If he has a fever, he will feel hot when you touch the inside of his back legs.

His eyes will have a tired look.

Don't ignore *symptoms.*

Ask someone to help you take your dog's temperature. Use a rectal thermometer. Shake down the mercury, dip the bulb end in vaseline or rub some soap on it, then insert it in the dog's anus. Let it stay for two minutes.

Normal   101° – 102°

High   103°

Subnormal   99°

If your dog's temperature is normal, the thermometer will read between 101 and 102 degrees. A temperature over 103 degrees or less than 100 degrees is equally dangerous.

TROUBLE SIGNS

You need help from your veterinarian if your dog:

has diarrhea repeatedly,
has a high temperature,
has a subnormal one, for long,
vomits repeatedly,
eats unusual things such as hair, wool, dirt or animal drop-
    pings,
drinks an abnormal amount of water,
urinates frequently,
passes blood in either the urine or the stool,
has convulsions.

RULES FOR THE SICK ROOM

Keep your dog warm.

Keep him quiet.

Keep him away from other dogs.

If he has diarrhea, take away solid foods. Give "honey water" (1 teaspoonful of honey to 1 cup of warm water) three times a day.

If the stool is white and chalky, this means your dog is constipated. Give a mild laxative such as Milk of Magnesia, one teaspoonful to two tablespoonsful, depending upon the size of the dog.

Take your dog's temperature morning and night.

Report a change in temperature to your veterinarian.

When you put your dog back on regular food, do it gradually. Feed such things as raw meat, meat broth, rice and dairy products.

HOW TO GIVE MEDICINE

Put liquid medicine into a small bottle. Back your large dog into a corner or straddle him. Hold the dog's head up. Pull out the lower lip at the side to form a pocket. Pour in a little medicine at a time, then rub his throat to make him swallow.

Support the small dog by kneeling.

When you give your dog a pill, hold the pill between your first and second finger or between your thumb and your first finger, and poke it down your dog's throat as far as you can. When you take your hand away, pull the tongue gently toward you, then release it. Hold the dog's mouth closed and rub his throat until he swallows.

An easier way is to wrap the pill in a piece of meat or if it is hard, crumble it in some ice cream. Some pills are gelatin outside with a liquid inside, and you should make sure your dog swallows them whole.

Epsom salts are good for a swollen paw. With hot water, but not hot enough to burn, soak the paw three times a day for at least ten minutes.

If your dog claws at his face, see if something is caught between his teeth or in the back of his mouth. It could be a wire or a piece of string, perhaps even a bone.

If your dog has been in a dog fight, go over him carefully. Wash all wounds with disinfectant and check them daily. Dog bites become infected easily.

The purpose of a splint is to keep a broken bone from becoming more damaged. If your dog should break his leg, keep him quiet and the leg rigid until the bone can be reset.

Hornets and bees sting dogs as well as people. A good home treatment is an ice pack or household ammonia. If the dog has been stung severely, take him to the veterinarian as quickly as you can.

We hope it doesn't happen to your dog, but if he should be hit by a car, throw a blanket over him and muzzle him before you move him. A dog in pain may bite his very best friend.

Dogs swallow many things they should not. A teaspoonful of salt on the back of his tongue will make your dog vomit such things as part of a sponge, small metal objects or spoiled food.

If your dog swallows a chicken or fish bone or some other sharp object, such as a pin, feed bread soaked in water or give him some mashed potatoes—as much as the dog will eat. If you can't get him to the veterinarian immediately, continue the home treatment every two hours.

If you ever have to bandage your dog's paw, don't make the bandage too tight. Keep the paw dry and check at intervals for signs of the leg swelling. Rubbing the bandage with soap, or alum or bitter apple from your drugstore, might keep the dog from chewing it.

An Elizabethan collar will keep your dog from scratching at a sore ear or a spot on his face. To make the collar, you need cardboard, a pair of scissors, a shoestring or a piece of twine. Cut two over-lapping half circles from the cardboard, with an opening the size of the dog's neck. Punch holes and tie them together with the string. Your dog will look funny, but don't laugh AT him; laugh WITH him.

Does your dog cry when he scratches his ear? The ear may be infected. An ear with a sour odor and smelling of wax, needs veterinarian treatment.

A dog will drool when is hungry, but a bad tooth will cause saliva to drip from his mouth.

A runny nose but no fever, may mean your dog has caught a cold. Give him one aspirin (¼ to ½ if he is a small dog), keep him warm and quiet and watch for other signs of sickness.

If he swallows with difficulty, look at your dog's throat. If it is red and inflamed, this could be serious. See the veterinarian!

A cold, wet nose is usually a sign of good health. A hot, dry nose may indicate a fever. It is not uncommon, though, for a dog to have a cold nose and still be very sick. Rely on your thermometer.

Your dog doesn't have to be near a sick dog to catch a disease. Germs are carried on our hands, our clothing, our shoes, by insects and by the very air we breathe. This is why you must be careful to wash your hands and change your clothes if you have been near a dog that is sick.

Rectal thermometer

Boric Acid Solution (for eyes)

Tincture of iodine or metaphen (for wounds)

Milk of Magnesia (as a laxative)

Kaopectate (for diarrhea)

Aspirin (as a sedative and to fight fever)

Yellow Oxide of Mercury—2% (for eye injury)

Petroleum jelly (for thermometer and use on skin)

Suppositories (to aid in housebreaking, traveling)

Zonite or some other disinfectant (antiseptic)

Pearson's Creolin (for fleas and lice)

B.F.I. powder (for the ears)

Epsom salts (for sprains or paw injuries)

Skin ointment (as recommended by your veterinarian)

Gauze bandage

Cotton

Adhesive

Even the most gentle dog will bite when he is in pain. Sometimes dogs bite when they are being groomed. If for any reason you have to muzzle your dog, use a strip of cloth, a piece of gauze bandage or an old silk stocking to tie his mouth shut. This is how to do it:

Tie a knot on the top of his nose, then one under his chin, and finally, make a bow-knot on the back of his neck. Make sure his lip is not caught between his teeth.

HOW TO LIFT YOUR DOG

Lift your dog by holding him close. Support his chest with one arm and let him sit on your other arm. It hurts when you pull your dog up by his front legs or lift him by the skin on his neck. You might even injure him.

When a dog is tied, he gets restless and pulls on the leash. To keep your dog from tightening his knot, tie him like this. Then all you have to do is to slip the free end through the loop and pull.

HOW TO WEIGH YOUR DOG

You can weigh a dog in one of three ways. Weigh the very small puppy in a basket on the kitchen scale. Turn the adjusting knob to zero with the basket in place. While the puppy is in the basket, hold your hands near him so he can't fall out.

If you can pick up your dog, step on the bathroom scale and see what you weigh together. Subtract your weight from the total and you will have your dog's weight, just like that.

If your dog is large, train him to sit and stay on a scale with a flat platform. Who wants to lift a Saint Bernard?

[53]

After your puppy is past the chewing stage, give him a basket, a blanket or a pillow to sleep on, and place it where there is no draft. If he sleeps out of doors, raise the bed off the floor or the ground to keep it free of dampness.

Cedar shavings or sawdust make a good outdoor bed for short-haired dogs or for those whose coat lies flat. For long-haired breeds, such as Poodles or Maltese, shred papers or cover a pillow with a towel that will launder easily.

SWEATER? RAINCOAT?

Animals that live outdoors in winter grow their own fur coats. House pets live in heated buildings and ride in warm cars. If your dog is low-slung like the Dachshund, or if he is one of the Toy breeds, a coat or a sweater will protect his tummy from snow and from rainy sidewalks. If you own a Poodle and take away nature's protection through clipping, he needs a coat to keep him warm.

CAR SICKNESS

There is no magic cure for car sickness, but these things might keep your dog from getting sick every time he goes in the car:

Take him riding while he is still a puppy.
Take him riding every day and on short trips.
Don't feed him before you take him riding.
Leave windows partly open for air.
In persistent cases, allow the dog to sit in a parked car.
Feed him in the car.

If he still gets sick, a sedative or a sea-sickness pill might help.

While riding, if you think your dog is going to get sick, hold his head UP, rub his throat and make him swallow.

Some people believe car sickness is caused by loss of balance. This centers in the ears. Cotton in the ears or covering them in some way may help.

Don't be ashamed to use the word "bitch." This is the proper word for your female dog.

A bitch normally comes in "heat" or in "season" twice a year. This is the period when, if you breed her, she will have puppies.

A bitch's season lasts about three weeks. You will know when she comes in season because she will have a colored discharge.

If you don't want to raise a litter of puppies, keep her away from male dogs the full period of her season. If you breed her, keep her confined anyway.

It takes 63 days for a bitch to have puppies. Puppies are born blind. Their eyes open between ten days and two weeks.

DOG SHOWS

If you are wondering about dog shows, there are several kinds:

At an *All-Breed Show,* dogs are judged on their appearances.

At *Obedience Trials,* they are judged on how well they perform a series of working tests.

In *Field Trials,* sporting dogs are judged on what good hunters they are.

Specialty Shows are those in which only one breed is exhibited or only one event is held, such as an Obedience Trial.

For dog show purposes, all pure-bred dogs are divided into six Variety Groups:

SPORTING DOGS

Wirehaired Pointing Griffon
Pointer
German Shorthaired Pointer
Chesapeake Bay Retriever
Curly-Coated Retriever
Flat-Coated Retriever
Golden Retriever
Labrador Retriever
English Setter
Gordon Setter
Irish Setter

American Water Spaniel
Brittany Spaniel
Clumber Spaniel
American Cocker Spaniel
English Cocker Spaniel
English Springer Spaniel
Field Spaniel
Irish Water Spaniel
Sussex Spaniel
Welsh Springer Spaniel
Weimaraner

SPORTING breeds are used for hunting and retrieving birds.

HOUND DOGS

Afghan
Basenji
Basset
Beagle
Black & Tan Coon-hound
Bloodhound
Borzoi
Dachshund
Scottish Deerhound

American Foxhound
English Foxhound
Greyhound
Harrier
Norwegian Elkhound
Otterhound
Saluki
Whippet
Irish Wolfhound

HOUND breeds track other animals.

WORKING DOGS

Alaskan Malamute
Belgian Malinois
Belgian Sheepdog
Belgian Tervuren
Bernese Mountain Dog
Bouvier des Flandres
Boxer
Briard
Bullmastiff
Rough Collie
Smooth Collie
Doberman Pinscher
German Shepherd
Great Dane
Great Pyrenees

Komondor
Kuvasz
Mastiff
Newfoundland
Old English Sheepdog
Puli
Rottweiler
Saint Bernard
Samoyed
Giant Schnauzer
Standard Schnauzer
Shetland Sheepdog
Siberian Husky
Cardigan Welsh Corgi
Pembroke Welsh Corgi

WORKING breeds were originally bred to perform special services such as herding sheep or acting as guard dogs.

TERRIERS

Airedale
Australian
Bedlington
Border
Bull Terrier (both Colored and White)
Cairn
Dandie Dinmont
Smooth Fox
Wire Fox
Irish

Kerry Blue
Lakeland
Manchester
Norwich
Miniature Schnauzer
Scottish
Sealyham
Skye
Staffordshire
Welsh
West Highland White

TERRIER breeds are experts when it comes to catching animals that live under the ground.

TOY DOGS

Affenpinscher
Chihuahua (long coat)
Chihuahua (smooth coat)
English Toy Spaniel
    (Blenheim and Prince
    Charles)
English Toy Spaniel
    (King Charles and Ruby)
Brussels Griffon
Italian Greyhound
Japanese Spaniel

Maltese
Toy Manchester Terrier
Papillon
Pekingese
Miniature Pinscher
Pomeranian
Toy Poodle
Pug
Shih Tzu
Silky Terrier
Yorkshire Terrier

As you can tell from the name, TOY breeds are small dogs.

NON-SPORTING DOGS

Boston Terrier
Bulldog
Chow Chow
Dalmatian
French Bulldog

Keeshond
Lhasa Apsos
Miniature Poodle
Standard Poodle
Schipperke

Breeds that do not fall into a special classification are placed in the NON-SPORTING GROUP.

HOW A DOG BECOMES A
BREED CHAMPION

Dog show classes are divided into six classifications:

The Puppy Class

The Puppy Class is for dogs under a year old.

The Novice Class

The Novice Class is for dogs that have never won first prize except as a puppy.

The American-Bred Class

Dogs entered in the American-Bred Class must be born in the United States.

The Bred-by-Exhibitor Class

Dogs shown in the Bred-by-Exhibitor Class must be bred and owned by the person who handles the dog, or by a member of the family.

The Open Class

The Open Class is open to all dogs and, except for puppies, dogs born in other countries must be shown in the Open Class.

The Winners Class

The Winners Class is for those dogs that win first prize in the classes mentioned above.

The Puppy, Novice, American-Bred, Bred-by-Exhibitor, Open and Winners Classes are also divided by sex.

THE AMERICAN KENNEL CLUB
CHAMPIONSHIP CERTIFICATE

This certifies that

BETSWORTH JUDY VAN BUREN

ENGLISH SETTER   SA-142534

owned by _____ BETSWORTH KENNELS

having completed the requirements for a championship

on ___ JUNE 22, 1963 ___ *has been officially recorded as*

CHAMPION

by The American Kennel Club

J.B. Everett
Secretary

[63]

(*Dogs*)			(*Bitches*)	
Puppy			Puppy	
Novice			Novice	
American-Bred	} *Winners Dog*		American-Bred	} *Winners Bitch*
Bred-by Exhibitor			Bred-by-Exhibitor	
Open			Open	

The dog and bitch that take first prize in the Winners Class win points toward their championships. The number of points depends upon the number of dogs and bitches shown that day. The dog and bitch that win second prize in the Winners Class receive a ribbon that says *Reserve Winners.*

When a dog or bitch receives 15 championship points under at least three different judges, with two of the wins being major ones (three points or more), the dog becomes a champion of his breed. The word Champion or the letters CH. appear before the dog's name. He remains a champion for life.

The Winners Dog and the Winners Bitch, together with the dogs that are already champions, then compete for *Best of Breed* (or *Best of Variety,* if the breed has more than one size or one color.)

Following Best of Breed competition, the Winners Dog and Winners Bitch are judged against each other for the *Best of Winners* ribbon. (Of course, if either has won *Best of Breed,* he or she is automatically Best of Winners.) The Best of Winners is entitled to the highest number of championship points earned by either sex of the breed.

The final award is called *Best of Opposite Sex.* If a male wins *Best of Breed* or *Best of Variety,* a female is named *Best of Opposite Sex.* If a female wins, a male takes home the red and white *Best of Opposite Sex* ribbon.

All Best of Breed or Best of Variety winners are eligible to enter their variety group to compete against the other Best of Breed or Best of Variety winners in their group. There are four placings in each group and the ribbons are the same as in the classes: blue is first, red is second, yellow is third, and white is fourth.

A Best of Breed or Best of Variety winner is not required to enter his respective group, but if the dog enters and wins his group, he *must* compete for BEST DOG IN SHOW.

HOW A DOG IS NAMED
BEST IN SHOW

It is possible for a judge to select one breed of dog as being better than another breed by comparing each dog to the written standard for his breed. For example, the Chihuahua in the Toy Group is judged against the "perfect" Chihuahua; the Pomeranian in the same group is judged against the "perfect" Pomeranian. When the first place winners of the six Variety Groups compete against one another and the judge selects a single dog as Best In Show, in his opinion, that dog came closest to the standard for his breed on that day. The ribbon is a beautiful red, white and blue rosette.

BOXER

(Every breed has a standard of excellence.)

HEAD in correct relationship to skull; never too small; clean with neither deep wrinkles nor dewlap; typical, unique

EYES dark brown; not too small nor protruding nor deep-set; expression of energy and intelligence; dark rims

STOP distinct but neither forced into forehead nor sloping; furrow between eyes

NOSE broad, black, slightly turned up somewhat higher than muzzle; nostrils broad

MUZZLE square, powerfully developed in length, breadth, depth; not pointed, narrow, short, shallow

JAWS wide; lower protrudes beyond upper; bends slightly upward; upper broad where attached to skull; under-shot; bite powerful, sound

CHEEKS well-developed, no protrusion

MASK dark, confined to muzzle; in distinct contrast to head color; a REQUIRED trait

UPPER ARM long, forms right angle to shoulder blade

CHEST deep, reaching to elbows; depth, half of height at withers

FORELEGS straight, parallel; bones strong, firmly joined

FEET small, tightly arched toes (cat's paws); hard soles; turning neither in nor out

COAT short, shiny, smooth, tight to body

SIZE: Weight, males, at 23" height, weight over 66 lbs.; females at 22", weight 62 lbs. Height, males, 22"-24" at withers, not under; females, 21"-23" at withers, not over

BODY well-balanced; medium-sized; square in profile, sturdy, short; muscular, clean, powerfully developed; skin taut; equipped for speed, never racy

LIPS upper, thick, padded; lower edge rests on ledge of lower lip; lower must be perceptible viewed from front; teeth, tongue must not show when mouth is closed

TEETH sound, powerful bite; lower incisors in straight line; upper, slightly rounded; middle incisors do not project. This creates frontal width in both jaws, canine teeth widely separated. Upper corner incisors fit snugly back of lowers

SKULL top slightly arched; occiput not too pronounced

EARS high set, clipped to point, fairly long, shell not too broad; carried erect

NECK round, length ample; strong, muscular, clean; no dewlap; distinctly marked nape, elegant arch

SHOULDERS distinctly marked, clearly defined

BACK short, straight, broad, muscular; withers clearly defined; loins short, muscular. Croup slightly sloped, broad

ELBOWS not too close, yet not off too far

RIBS well-arched, extending far to rear

UNDERLINE graceful curve

PASTERNS clearly defined, short; slight slant but almost perpendicular to ground

TAIL—set-high rather than too deep; clipped; carried upward

PELVIS long; broad in females

THIGHS broad, curved; breech muscula-tion strongly developed; long

HINDQUARTER JOINTS well-angulated; in balance with forequarters; thighs broad, curved; breech musculation strongly developed

HIND LEGS straight, viewed from rear; hocks clean, not distended; hock joints per-pendicular to ground

FEET strong pads; rear toes slightly longer than front, catlike

COLOR fawn, in various shades from light yellow to dark deer red; brindle should have black stripes on fawn background; stripes clearly defined, cov-ering top of body; white marking not rejected

DISQUALIFICATIONS—white or black ground color, or entirely white or black or any color other than fawn or brindle. (White markings allowed but must not exceed one-third of ground color)

Reprinted by special permission from Popular Dogs magazine, Philadelphia

HOW A DOG BECOMES
AN OBEDIENCE CHAMPION

Obedience degrees appear *after* the dog's name.

C.D. means *Companion Dog*
C.D.X. means *Companion Dog Excellent*
U.D. means *Utility Dog*
U.D.T. means *Utility Dog Tracker*
T.D. means *Tracking Dog*

In the obedience classes, all breeds compete against one another. There are three classes, Novice, Open and Utility. There is also a Tracking Test, but this is not held at a dog show.

In order to win obedience degrees, a dog must receive a certain score; he must pass under different judges, and he must compete against other dogs. The exciting thing about obedience trials is that a dog that fails one day can win top honors the next.

REQUIREMENTS FOR THE
NOVICE CLASS (C.D. DEGREE)

Heel on Leash	35 Points
Stand for Examination	30 Points
Heel Free	45 Points
Recall	30 Points
Long Sit	30 Points
Long Down	30 Points
Maximum Total Score	200 Points

(Less Penalty for Misbehavior)

REQUIREMENTS FOR THE
OPEN CLASS (C.D.X. DEGREE)

Heel Free	40 Points
Drop on Recall	30 Points
Retrieve on Flat	25 Points
Retrieve over High Jump	35 Points
Broad Jump	20 Points
Long Sit	25 Points
Long Down	25 Points
Maximum Total Score	200 Points

(Less Penalty for Misbehavior)

REQUIREMENTS FOR
UTILITY CLASS

Scent Discrimination (leather) .... 30 Points
Scent Discrimination (metal) .... 30 Points
Directed Retrieve .... 30 Points
Seek Back .... 30 Points
Signal Exercise .... 35 Points
Directed Jumping .... 40 Points
Group Examination .... 35 Points

Maximum Total Score .... 200 Points

(Less Penalty for Misbehavior)

T.D. (TRACKING DOG)

The Tracking Test, held separately from a dog show, requires the dog to follow the scent of a stranger a quarter of a mile on a track that is one-half to two hours old. A Tracking Dog should be able to find a criminal or a lost person.

DOG SHOW RULES

Your dog must be over six months of age before you can enter him in a licensed dog show.

He must be pure-bred.

He must be registered or eligible for registration with the American Kennel Club.

He must have no disqualifying faults such as blindness, lameness or other faults set up by the Standard for the breed.

Your dog can't be dyed or have his color changed in any way.

Once you take your dog on the show ground, you must show him in all classes in which he is entered.

In obedience, your dog must work accurately, and you must handle him with care.

There are other rules pertaining to color, physical make-up, size, and temperament in obedience. Make certain you are familiar with all the rules before you enter your dog in a breed show or an obedience trial. Otherwise you may be told that your dog has been disqualified or that he does not pass in obedience.

Dog shows are run by Superintendents licensed by the American Kennel Club. Premium lists, mailed in advance, advertise the shows and tell who the judges will be. Money and trophies make up the awards. Kennel owners, veterinarians, or other people who work with dogs can tell you how to get your name on a mailing list so you will know when and where a dog show will be held.

Send for this booklet if you want to show your dog in a breed show.

Rules Applying to Registration and Dog Shows

Amended to October 15, 1963

THE AMERICAN KENNEL CLUB
Incorporated
New York, N. Y.

Send for this booklet if you want to show your dog in obedience trials. Both are available from the American Kennel Club, 51 Madison Avenue, New York, New York. In Canada, the Canadian Kennel Club, 667 Yonge Street, Toronto.

DOG SHOW RIBBONS

1st	2nd	3rd	4th	Winners
(Blue)	(Red)	(Yellow)	(White)	(Purple)

Note: The only ribbon that awards points toward a dog's championship, is the purple one.

Reserve Winners	Best of Winners	Best of Breed or Best of Variety	Best of Opposite Sex
(Purple & White)	(Blue & White)	(Purple & Gold)	(Red & White)

SANCTIONED MATCHES

Watch for these to come in your town. A sanctioned match is a show where, at little expense, one can find out if his dog is good enough to compete in a regular show or if he has had enough training to enter an obedience trial. A sanctioned match is run like a regular show, but wins do not count toward the dog's championship or toward his obedience degrees.

JUNIOR SHOWMANSHIP CLASSES

Junior Showmanship Classes are for young people. Different age groups from ten to sixteen compete for ribbons and prizes at almost every dog show. The awards are based on how well boys and girls show their dogs in the breed ring. This doesn't mean, however, that a young person can't exhibit his dog in a regular breed class or obedience trial where it is the dog that counts.

TRAVELING WITH YOUR DOG

Taking your dog with you on vacation this year? Prepare him now!

Train your dog to do his duties while on leash. Tell him, "Duties! Duties!" so he will hurry things up. If he is modest and slow to learn, fasten two leashes together or use a long rope.

Take your dog in the car as often as you can before you leave on vacation so he will learn to ride without getting sick.

Make him behave in the car. Tie him or threaten him with a small rolled magazine if he acts wild.

Make him wait for permission to leave the car.

Touring with Towser, distributed by the Gaines Dog Research Center, 250 Park Avenue, New York, N.Y., lists the hotels and motels all over the country that take dogs. There is a mailing fee for the booklet, but it is very useful.

BEFORE YOU LEAVE ON VACATION

Fasten your dog's license and rabies tags to his collar.

Carry a health certificate from your veterinarian.

In case your dog gets lost, hang another tag on his collar, giving your home address.

And REMEMBER! When you leave your dog in the car, it must be parked in the shade with windows partly open for air.

Here are some things the traveler may need; take as many as you can:

A collar and leash
A long line for exercise
A supply of dog food
A can opener
A mixing spoon
A feeding pan
A water thermos
Brush and comb
One or two towels
Your dog's blanket
Newspapers
A thermometer, in case you need to take your dog's temperature
Glycerine suppositories (to make him go to the bathroom)
Something for diarrhea
And, if there is room, a small dog crate or folding wire cage

If you are traveling by air, rail or sea, call the transportation authorities. Rules vary. For instance, you can rent a crate from certain air lines. With others, you have to furnish your own. And never, *never* attempt to ship a dog anywhere without a health certificate, and rabies shot if the country or state requires one.

A dog whose ancestry is known to consist of many generations of the same breed, with no mixture of blood from any other breeds, is a *pure-bred*. Don't call your dog a "thorough-bred."

A "police" dog is a dog that does police work, such as guarding or sentry duty. This is not another name for the German Shepherd dog, or any other breed.

A "registered" dog is a dog that is on record at the American Kennel Club. One eligible for registration has not been registered himself but his parents have.

Even though a dog has been inoculated against distemper and hepatitis, he can still catch these diseases. Remember to give your dog a booster shot once a year. When your dog gets old, limit stairs. Give him a warm place to sleep, and overlook his grouchiness. A regular physical examination will tell you if your dog needs a special diet, and through your kind words and loving pats, he will know you still love him in his old age.

Never reach to pat a dog you don't know. If a dog wants to be friendly, he will come to you.

Never run or scream when a dog growls or barks at you; stand still. In a low, demanding voice, say, "Go home!" or "Scat!" When you move on, continue slowly.

Never reach for a frightened dog. Using the leash or a piece of rope, make a noose and drop it slowly over the dog's head. If he is a small dog and you want to pick him up, pull the leash forward and hold it tight. Lift him by reaching under his hindquarters.

SOME INTERESTING FACTS

Do you know:

Silver Poodles are born black.

Dalmatians are born white and spots appear later.

Greyhounds can run as fast as 45 miles an hour.

The Basenji doesn't bark; he chortles.

This is called "pointing," a dog's way of saying, "Something is hiding in those bushes."

Working dogs were bred to perform a special service.

Borzoi is another name for the Russian Wolfhound.

Schipperke, in Flemish, means "little Captain."

THESE ARE THE PROPER NAMES FOR THE PARTS OF YOUR DOG'S BODY

DOG PROFESSIONS—

If you want to work with dogs when you grow up:

Dog Artist	Kennel Assistant
Dog Beautician	Kennel Manager
Dog Breeder	Manager of a boarding kennel
Dog Broker (one who imports and exports dogs)	Pet Shop Owner
Dog Food Salesman	Professional Handler
Dog Judge	Professional Trainer
Dog Photographer	Superintendent of Dog Shows
Dog Sitter (for city dogs)	Supplier of Dog Accessories
Dog Walker (service for city dogs)	Training Class Instructor
Dog Writer	Veterinarian
Humane Society Worker	Veterinarian's Assistant

Breed ___Dachshund___

Name ___Scoop Von Snap Cragel.___

Color and markings ___Black & Tan___

Sex ___Male___

Birthday ___30___ ___April___ ___1973___
           day   month   year

State License number _____

American Kennel Club number (if registered) _____

Where purchased _____

Date of purchase ___June 25, 1973___

PHOTOGRAPH

PEDIGREE

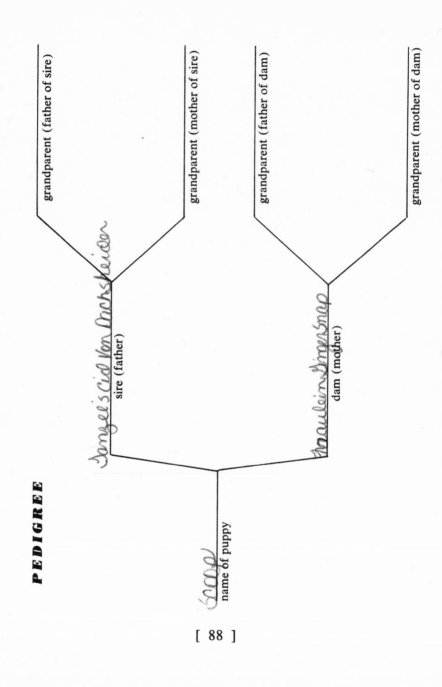

grandparent (father of sire)

grandparent (mother of sire)

grandparent (father of dam)

grandparent (mother of dam)

Sorrel's Cid Von Dachsheim
sire (father)

Mauliens Dingerbnap
dam (mother)

name of puppy

SHOTS

Distemper

_____ _____
date　　　　　　　　　　Veterinarian

_____ _____
date　　　　　　　　　　Veterinarian

Hepatitis

_____ _____
date　　　　　　　　　　Veterinarian

_____ _____
date　　　　　　　　　　Veterinarian

Booster

_____ _____
date　　　　　　　　　　Veterinarian

_____ _____
date　　　　　　　　　　Veterinarian

_____ _____
date　　　　　　　　　　Veterinarian

Rabies

_____ _____
date　　　　　　　　　　Veterinarian

_____ _____
date　　　　　　　　　　Veterinarian

Worming

_____ _____
date　　　　　　　　　　Kind

_____ _____
date　　　　　　　　　　Kind

[89]

Important dates to remember (if female)

When in season 1_____

2_____

3_____

4_____

5_____

6_____

Important telephone numbers

Local Veterinarian _____

Local Police _____

Local S.P.C.A. _____

SHOW RECORD

OBEDIENCE RECORD

Dogs age faster than humans do. You can roughly judge how old your dog is in comparison to man by the table below:

Dog's Age	Man's Age
6 Months	10 Years
8 Months	13 Years
10 Months	14 Years
12 Months	15 Years
18 Months	20 Years
2 Years	24 Years
4 Years	32 Years
6 Years	40 Years
8 Years	48 Years
10 Years	56 Years
12 Years	64 Years
14 Years	72 Years
16 Years	80 Years
18 Years	88 Years
20 Years	96 Years
21 Years	100 Years

OTHER BOOKS BY BLANCHE SAUNDERS

Training You to Train Your Dog
The New Standard Book of Dog Care and Training (with Jeannette Cross)
The Complete Book of Dog Obedience
The Complete Novice Obedience Course
The Complete Open Obedience Course
The Complete Utility Obedience Course (with Tracking)
Dog Training for Boys and Girls